Kids Voyage to North America

AN INTRODUCTION TO THIRD LARGEST
CONTINENT OF THE WORLD

Judy Winters

Copyright © 2022 Judy Winters

No part of this publication may be reproduced, stored in a retrieval system, or transmitted in any form or by any means, electronic, mechanical, photocopying, recording, scanning, or otherwise except as permitted by prior written permission of the Author and Publisher.
Limit of Liability/ Disclaimer of warranty: Author and Publisher make no representations or warranties with respect to the accuracy and completeness of the contents of this work and specifically disclaim all warranties, including without limitation warranties of fitness for a particular purpose. No warranty may be created or extended by sales or promotional materials. The advice and strategies contained herein may not be suitable for every situation. Information presented in this book is put together by the author through commonly available knowledge and information available in the area of public domain. This work is sold with the understanding that the author and publisher is not engaged in rendering medical, legal, or other professional advice or services. If professional assistance is required, the services of a competent professional person should be sought. Neither the author nor the publisher shall be liable for damages arising herefrom. The fact that an individual, organization, or website is referred to in this work as a citation and/or potential source of further information does not mean that the Author or the Publisher endorses the information the individual, organization, or website may provide or recommendations they/ it may make. Further, readers should be aware that the Websites listed in this work may have changed or disappeared between when this work was written and when it is read.

All artistic elements used in covers and interiors for this work have been designed by the Designer/ Author/ Publisher/ Editor through their paid subscription to online design tools and resources like Canva™, Creative Fabrica™ using their custom templates, and graphics.

This book belongs to

....

Note to Supervising Adults

Thank you for choosing this book.

This book is written with the intent to introduce kids to North America. It starts with introducing the kids to the concept of the Earth & Continents. Book, then gradually shifts focus to North America.

The author starts with the big picture and then breaks it down into logical components so that:

- The child is able to co-relate the concepts
- The child is introduced to new concepts.
- Curiosity is raised and the child tries to find answers to some of the questions that arise

While this book attempts to share basic information about North America & countries there-in, it is requested that you inspire the child to find more about the continent and nations in it as a supervising adult.

Artist Impression – Distance & Boundaries Not to Scale

Earth is the wonderful planet that we live on and call home.

Earth is part of the "Solar System".

Earth is the third planet from the Sun in our Solar system. It takes 365 days to complete one orbit or a circle around Sun.

Earth is the fifth largest planet. It is covered by land and mostly by water.

The moon revolves around Earth and takes 24 hours to complete one orbit around it.

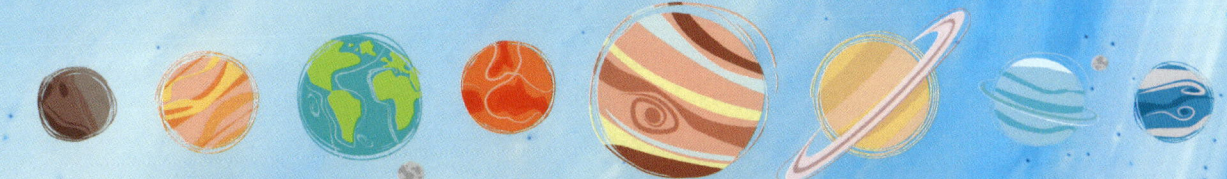

Earth has seven landmasses known as "Continents" surrounded by large bodies of water, Oceans.

There are seven continents and five oceans on Earth.

These continents were joined together, a long time back, before breaking away and getting separated from each other.

The seven continents are Asia, Africa, North America, South America, Europe, Australia, and Antarctica.

Each continent consists of more than one country that are joined together.

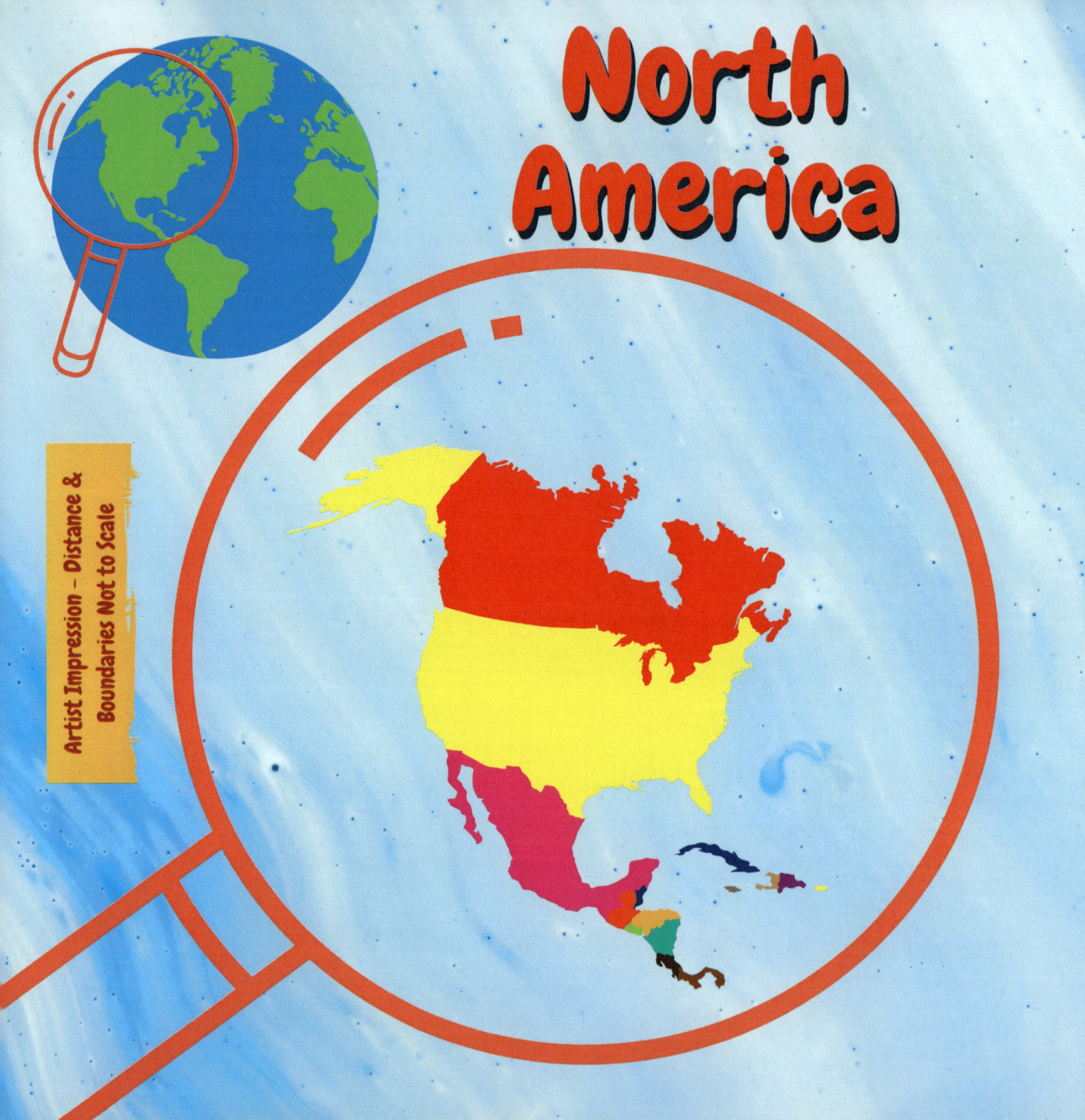

The continent of North America is entirely situated in the northern hemisphere and is almost located within the western hemisphere.

North America is the third largest continent in size after Asia and Africa.

The Arctic Ocean borders it to the north, The Atlantic Ocean to the east, The Pacific Ocean to the west, and to the southeast by South America and the Caribbean Sea.

It covers 17% of the total Earth's land area and 8% of the world's population lives here.
North America is the fourth largest continent in terms of population.

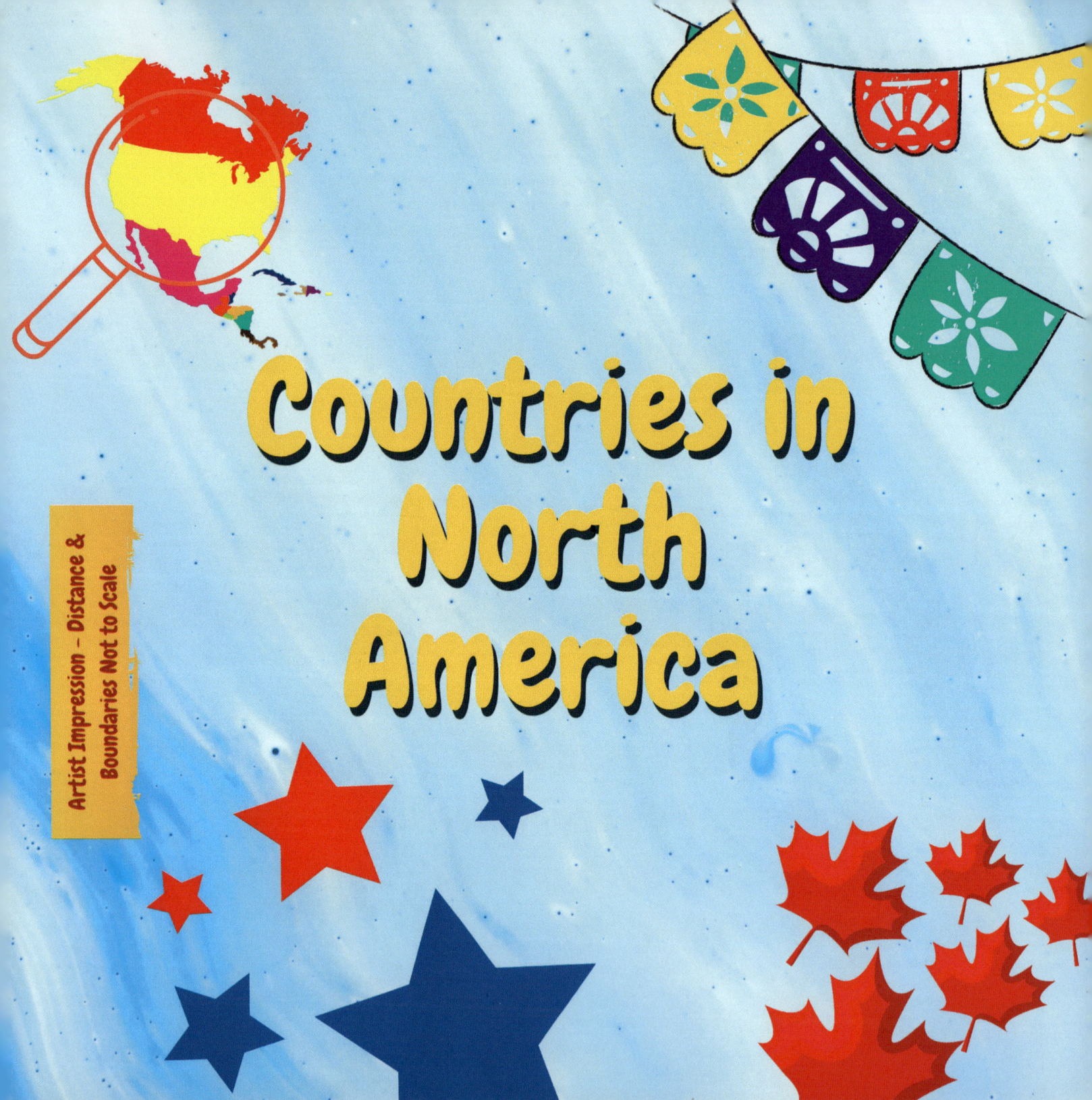

North America has 23 countries with more than half a billion people living in it.

The USA is the most populous country and Mexico City is the most populous city in North America.

Canada is the largest country by area whereas Saint Kitts & Nevis are the smallest.

Canada, the United States, and Mexico make up the largest part of the continent of North America.

Central America is also part of North America. It has countries like Nicaragua, Panama, & Costa Rica.

Islands, including the West Indies and Greenland, are also associated with North America.

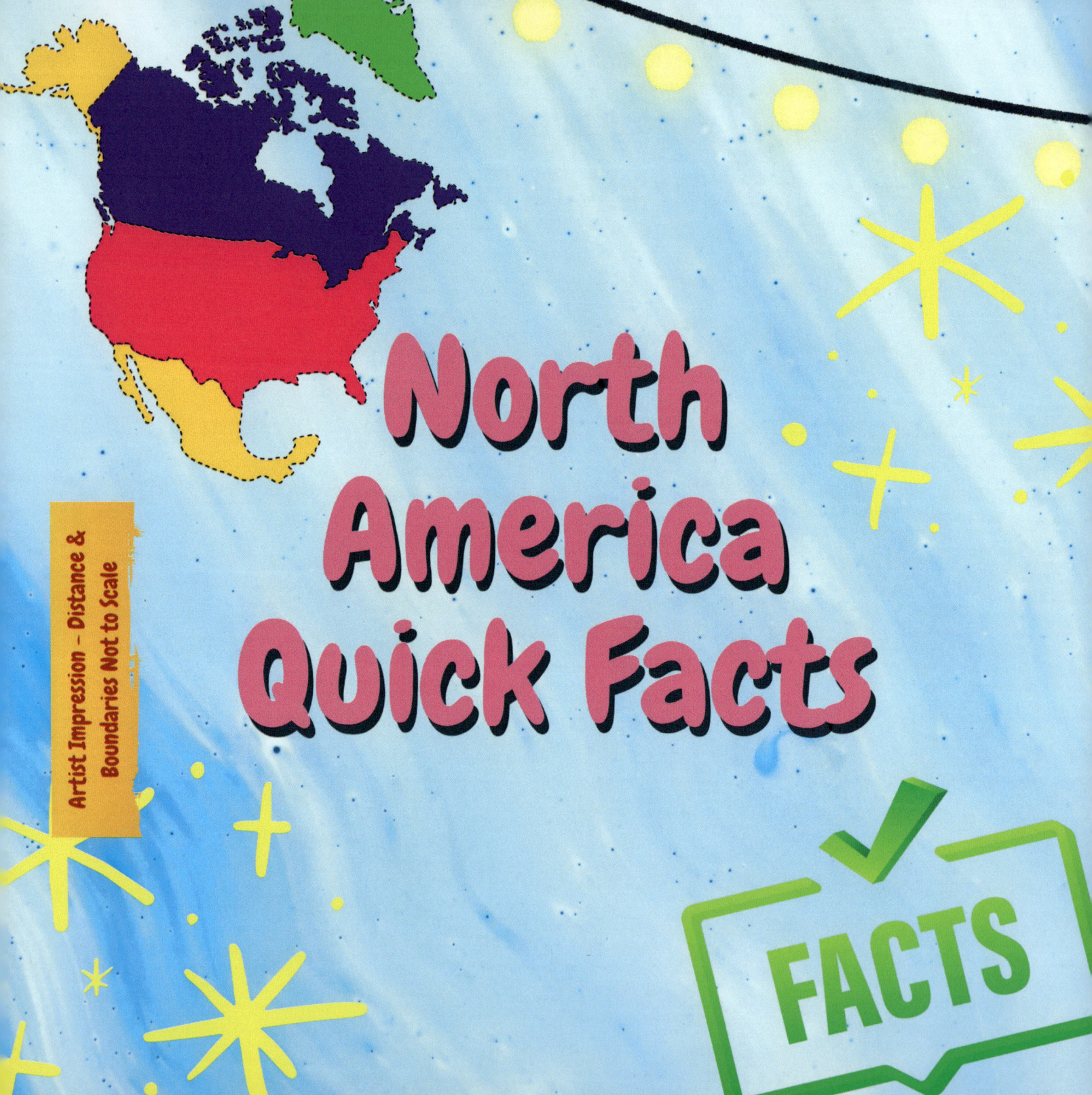

- **Land Mass:** 24,680,330 square kilometres (or 95,29,130 square miles)
- **Countries:** 23
- **Largest Island:** Greenland
- **Largest Lake:** Lake Superior is 82,100 square kilometers (31,700 square miles) in area
- **Largest river system:** Mississippi
- **Longest River:** Missouri River
- **Highest Peak:** USA's Denali rises to 6,168 meters above sea level
- **Hottest and lowest point:** Death Valley, located in the Mojave Desert, California.

North America has a large number of tourist attractions. Some of the places that attract people from all over the world are:

- New York City (USA) for its museums and shopping
- California (USA) for its amazing beaches perfect for surfing
- Niagra Falls (The USA and Canada) for its awe-inspiring views
- Las Vegas (USA) for its entertainment options, and popular shows
- Florida (USA) for its beaches and theme parks especially World Disney World

- **Los Angeles (USA)** for its studio tours and iconic Hollywood sign
- **Yucatan peninsula (Mexico)** for Mayan ruins and paradise beaches
- **Hawaii (USA)** for its natural beauty, volcanic islands, and breathtaking beaches
- **Rocky Mountains (The USA and Canada)** for skiing and winter sports
- **Grand Canyon (USA)** for hiking and nature experiences
- **Caribbean islands** for beaches, watersports, and nature trails

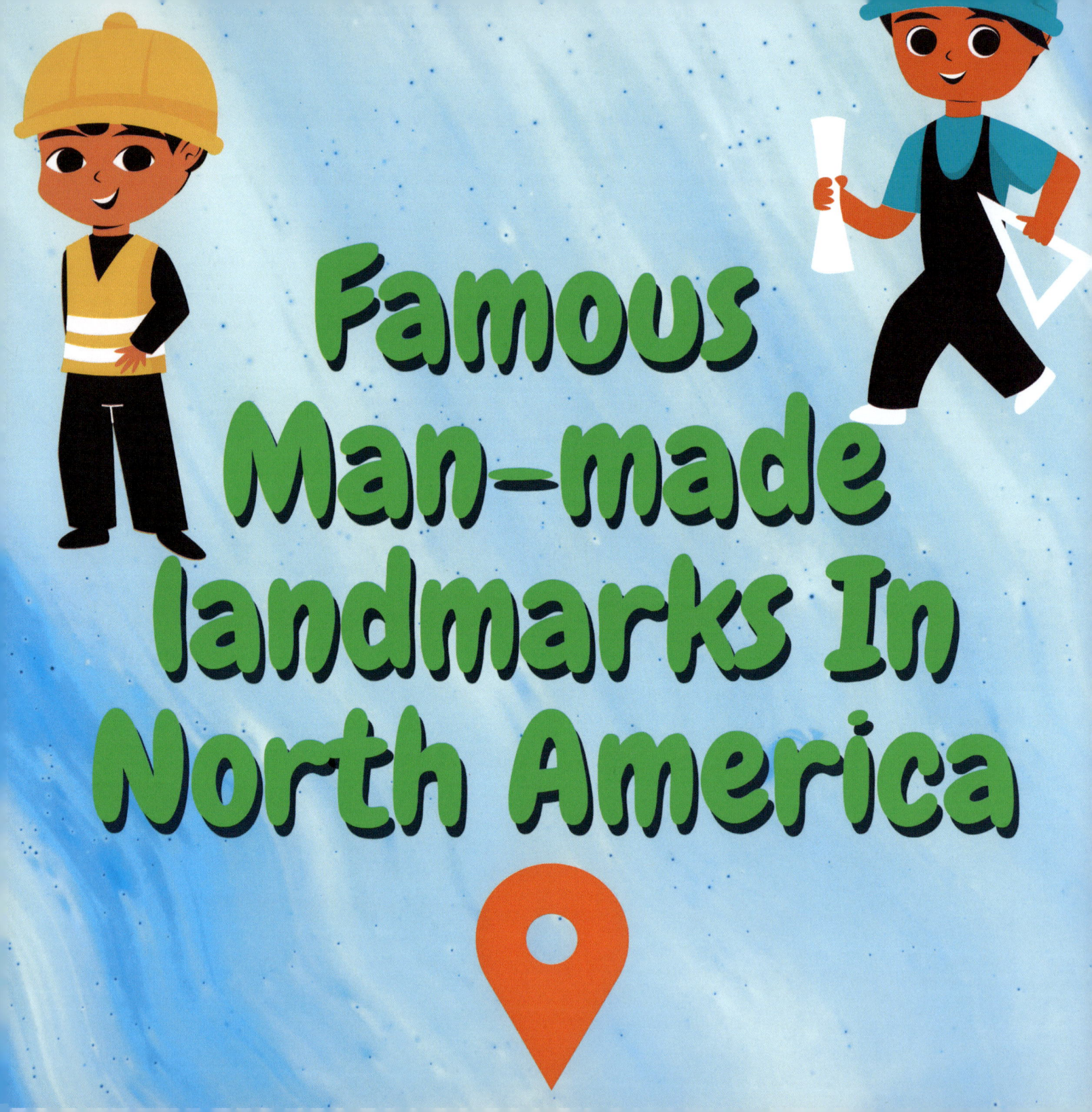
Famous Man-made landmarks In North America

Some of the man-made landmarks that are very popular with tourists are:
- Statue of Liberty, USA
- Empire State Building, USA
- Golden Gate Bridge, USA
- Chichen Itza, Mexico
- Capitol Building and The Mall, USA
- Mt. Rushmore, USA
- Hoover Dam, USA
- CN Tower, Canada
- Washington Monument, USA
- Panama Canal

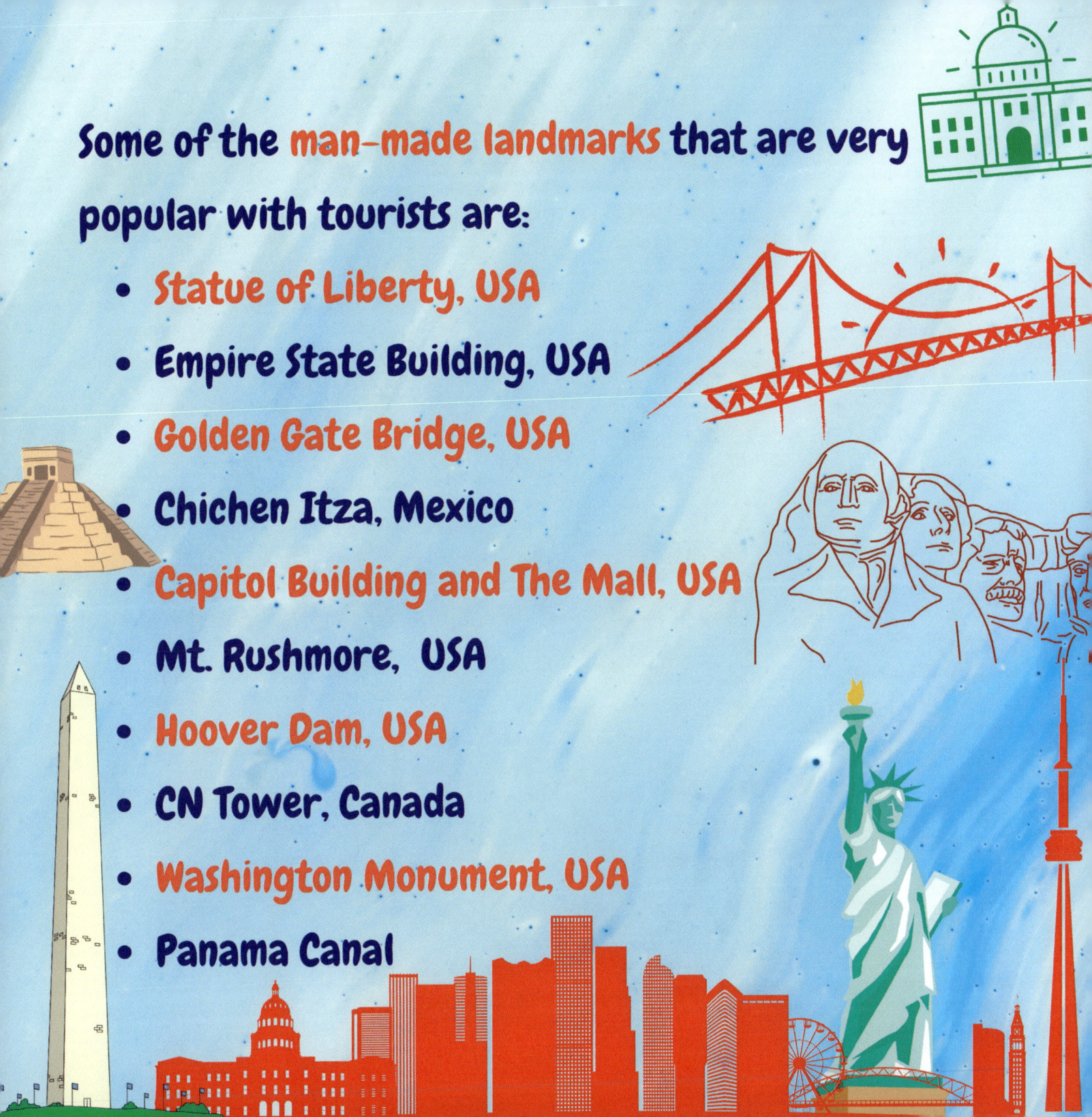

Major Cities In North America

Some of the major cities in North America are:

- Mexico City, Mexico
- New York City, USA
- Los Angeles, USA
- Chicago, USA
- Toronto, Canada
- Houston, USA
- Ecatepec de Morelos, Mexico
- Montreal, Canada
- Philadelphia, USA
- Guadalajara, Mexico

People of North America

North America was originally inhabited by Native Americans who are believed to have migrated here almost 15000 years ago by crossing a land bridge.

It was a Viking, Leif Eriksson, who is believed to be the first European to visit North America. He landed in what is now Canada in about 1000 CE. However, the Vikings did not make any permanent settlements.

It was only after an Italian explorer and navigator, Christopher Columbus, introduced the Americas to Western Europe in 1492 that Europeans started arriving to North America in numbers

People of North America

Europeans started to explore that continent and establish colonies. In general,

–the Spanish took control of the southern part of the continent (today's Mexico and Central America)

–the French settled in the northern part of the continent (today's Canada)

–the English settled in the middle (present-day United States).

Today, people from every corner of the globe live in the continent of North America, making it a 'melting pot' of inhabitants, traditions, and cultures.

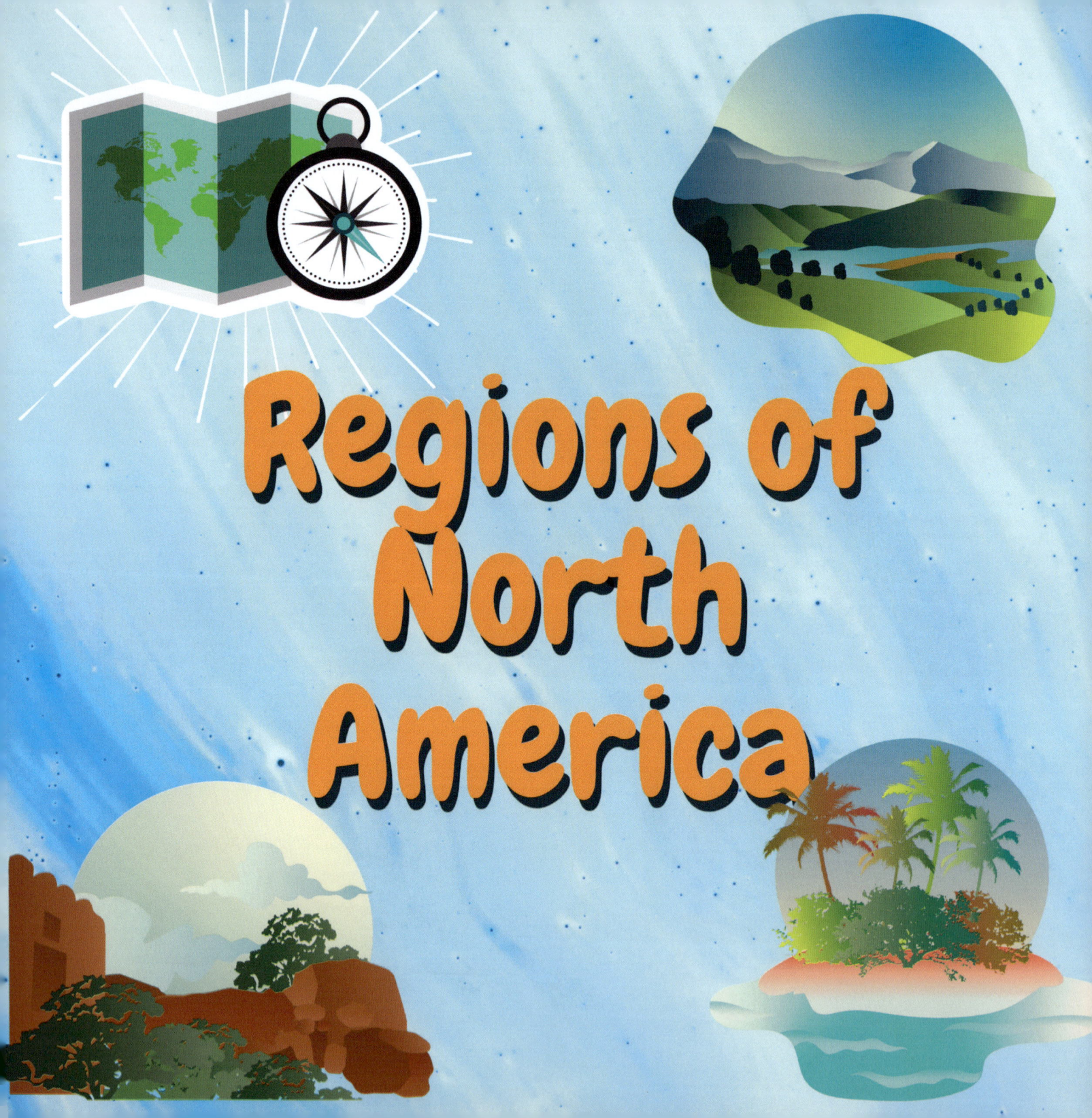

There are five chief regions in North America based on their geography.

These are Mountainous west, Great Plains, Canadian Shield, Eastern region, and the Caribbean.

In the western part of the continent, there are huge mountains including the Rocky Mountains in the United States and Sierra Madre mountain range in Mexico.

In the middle part of the continent, you'll find the great plains of the United States and Canada.

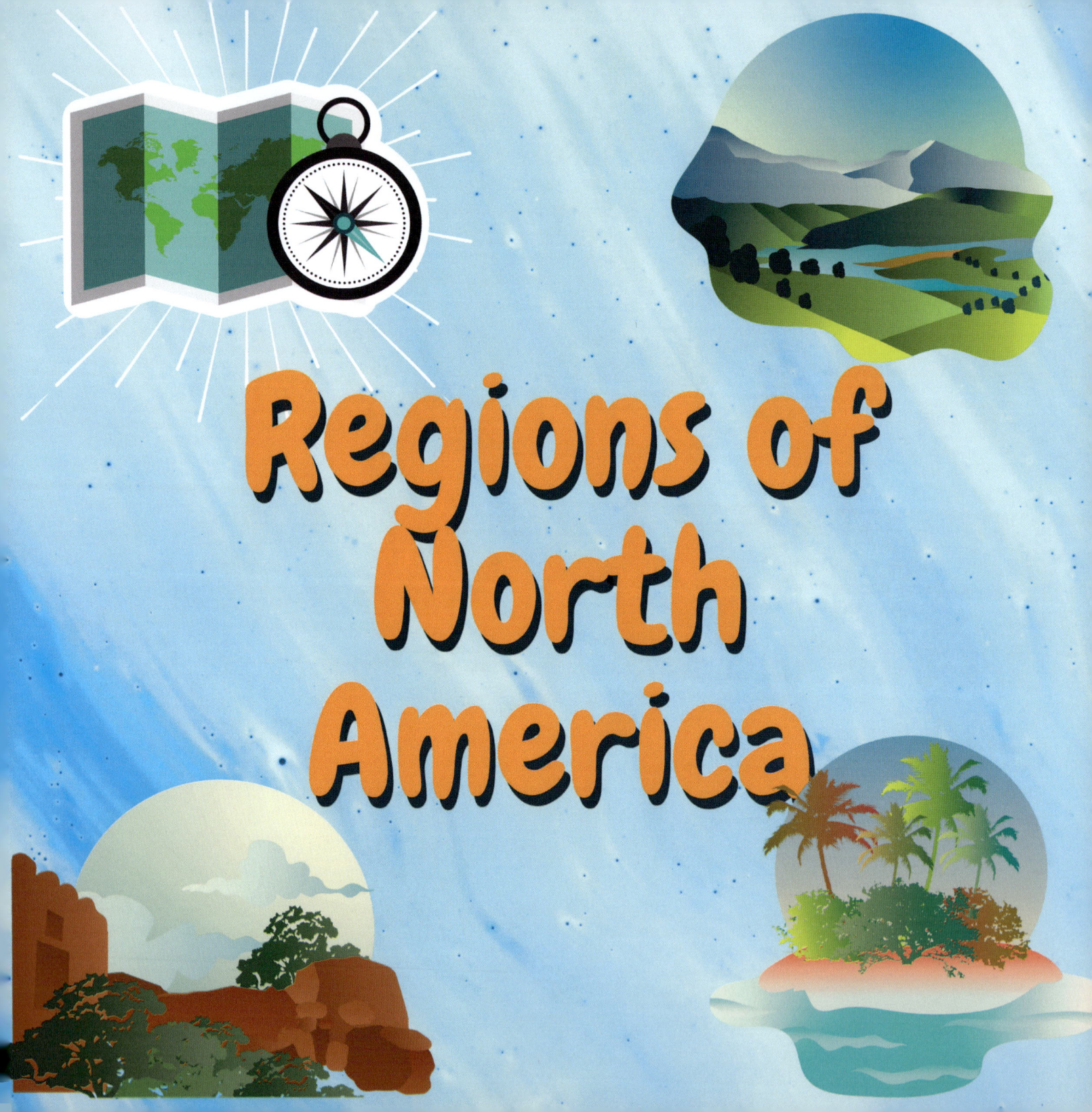

In the northern part, you will find the Canadian shield – a hilly region of lakes and swamps that stretches across northern Canada.

The eastern regions of North America contain everything from mountains to wetlands.

The fifth region is the Caribbean, which is, home to more than 700 islands, islets, reefs, and caves.

Even further south is Central America. It has some of the most beautiful rainforests and exotic animals.

Most of North America has a mild climate, with warm summers, cold winters, and moderate rainfall.

However, much of Alaska and northern Canada have bitterly cold winters and short, cool summers.

Parts of the southwestern United States and northwestern Mexico are very dry, with regions of desert and semi-desert.

Central America has hot weather and heavy rainfall throughout the year.

With so many diverse ecosystems, there are a variety of animals that live in North America.

Large water bodies surround North America; hence, the marine diversity is broad too.

In its cold regions, you will find mammals like Polar Bears and Moose.

In mountains, swamps, and plains you will find everything from Pumas to Crocodiles.

Deserts are famous for its wildlife like rattlesnakes and mammals.

In hot regions closer to the equator, like Mexico, you will find animals like armadillos, anteaters, and unique tamandua. You may also find Alligators, snakes, wild pigs, colorful birds, and monkeys in the warmer regions.

Other animals native to North America include bighorn sheep, mountain goats, Bison, Scorpions, Pronghorns, groundhogs, crocodiles, American bald eagle, and the elk. There are also bobcats, lynx, coyotes, wolves, and bears. Deer thrive in many areas, while squirrels, rabbits, and raccoons have started co-existing with the human population.

The mountainous parts of North America contain large areas of thick forests. Douglas fir, redwood, pine, and spruce trees grow along the northern Pacific Coast.

Tropical hardwood forests grow in Mexico and Central America.

Few plants grow in the desert and cold north.

Prairies form a belt between forest and desert, mainly on the Great Plains of the central part of the continent.

More About North America

- It is believed that North America is named after the Italian explorer, Amerigo Vespucci
- North America is the only continent that has each type of climate
- Mexico City in Mexico is the city with the maximum population in North America
- Greenland, the biggest island on the planet, is located in North America
- The lowest point on the continent is Death Valley. It holds the record for being the hottest and driest region on the planet

- Maximum number of Olympic medals in the world so far have been won by the athletes of North America
- It is the largest exporter of wheat in the world
- Cuba, a country in North America, is the world's largest exporter of sugar and is known as the world's sugar bowl
- Canada and USA have the longest land border in the world with 8,893 km/ 5,526 miles
- There is no landlocked country in North America!

- The first "skyscrapers" were built in Chicago/USA as early as the 1880s.
- New York, USA has still the second-most skyscrapers in a city! Most skyscrapers are in Hong Kong with more than 300 skyscrapers that are taller than 150 m
- Colonial Creek Falls in Washington State are the highest waterfalls in the continental USA. However, Oloupena Falls in Hawaii are unofficially named North America's highest waterfalls with a drop of 900 m/ 2,952 ft.

- Mauna Kea on the island of Hawaii/USA is the second highest mountain island in the world.
- The Rockies or the Rocky Mountains are among the longest mountain ranges in the world. Mount Elbert in Colorado/USA is the highest peak of the Rocky Mountains.
- Mammoth Cave in Kentucky has been recognised as the world's longest cave system with more than 650 km/ 405 miles of passageways.

Note from Author

Thank you for your purchase. Hope you, and your child enjoyed reading it and now your kid knows about North America better.

If you liked this book, request you to share your feedback on Amazon. Your Amazon rating and review will help me reach more kids.

For any suggestions to improve, you may email me at judywintersreads@gmail.com

God Bless!

Judy Winters

More from Judy Winters

KIDS VOYAGE TO SEVEN CONTINENTS

Scan QR Code To Buy Now!

Click The Link To Buy Now!

https://amzn.to/3xAPGEC!

Printed in Great Britain
by Amazon